I0814876

BEST OF THE SUPER BOWL

BIGGEST STARS OF THE SUPER BOWL

BY DAVID J. CLARKE

SportsZone

An Imprint of Abdo Publishing
abdobooks.com

abdobooks.com

Published by Abdo Publishing, a division of ABDO, PO Box 398166, Minneapolis, Minnesota 55439.

Printed in the United States of America, North Mankato, Minnesota.
102024
012025

Cover Photo: Focus on Sport/Getty Images (left); Focus on Sport/Getty Images Sport/Getty Images (center); Cooper Neill/Getty Images Sport/Getty Images (right)
Interior Photos: Focus On Sport/Getty Images, 4, 6, 8, 28; Jon Soohoo/Getty Images Sport/Getty Images, 10; Jeff Haynes/AFP/Getty Images, 11, 44–45; Gregory Shamus/Getty Images Sport/Getty Images, 13; Focus On Sport/Getty Images Sport/Getty Images, 14, 17, 18, 20, 37; Don Emmert/AFP/Getty Images, 22; Al Pereira/Getty Images Sport/Getty Images, 23; AP Images, 24–25; Bill Haber/AP Images, 27; Patrick Smith/Getty Images Sport/Getty Images, 31; Michael Owens/Getty Images Sport/Getty Images, 33; Nate Fine/Getty Images Sport/Getty Images, 34; Rick Stewart/Allsport/Getty Images Sport/Getty Images, 39; Timothy A. Clary/AFP/Getty Images, 41; Jim Davis/Boston Globe/Getty Images, 43; Paul Spinelli/AP Images, 45

Editor: Charlie Beattie
Series Designer: Jake Slavik

Library of Congress Control Number: 2024938341

Publisher's Cataloging-in-Publication Data

Names: Clarke, David J., author.
Title: Biggest stars of the Super Bowl / by David J. Clarke
Description: Minneapolis, Minnesota: ABDO Publishing, 2025 | Series: Best of the Super Bowl | Includes online resources and index.
Identifiers: ISBN 9781098295400 (lib. bdg.) | ISBN 9798384916406 (ebook)
Subjects: LCSH: Super Bowl--Records--Juvenile literature. | Football players--Juvenile literature. | American football--Juvenile literature. | National Football League--Juvenile literature. | Super Bowl superstars--Juvenile literature. | Football--United States--History--Juvenile literature.
Classification: DDC 796.332648--dc23

TABLE OF CONTENTS

STAR QUARTERBACKS

Terry Bradshaw wasn't always a great quarterback during the regular season. In his career with the Pittsburgh Steelers between 1970 and 1983, the rifle-armed passer tossed 212 touchdowns but also 210 interceptions. However, when the games got bigger, Bradshaw got better.

Often during his National Football League (NFL) career, fans and media members liked to joke that Bradshaw wasn't very smart. Opposing players even mocked him at times. Before Super Bowl XIII in January 1979, Dallas Cowboys linebacker Thomas "Hollywood" Henderson said that Bradshaw "couldn't spell 'cat' if you spotted him the 'c' and the 'a.'"

Bradshaw was furious. He'd already won the Super Bowl twice. He had been the league's Most Valuable Player (MVP) that season.

Terry Bradshaw looks to pass during Super Bowl X on January 18, 1976, against the Dallas Cowboys.

Terry Bradshaw threw for more than 300 yards in a game only seven times in his career, but two of those performances came in Super Bowls.

And he'd even beaten Henderson's Cowboys in Super Bowl X three years earlier. But now he had to prove himself all over again. On Pittsburgh's first drive, Bradshaw hit receiver John Stallworth on a 28-yard touchdown pass. Before the first half was over, Bradshaw had thrown two more scores, including a 75-yarder to Stallworth. At the time, that matched the record for the longest play in Super Bowl history.

Bradshaw added a fourth touchdown pass in the fourth quarter that made the score 35–17. After Pittsburgh held on to win 35–31, Bradshaw became the first quarterback to win the Super Bowl three times. He then told reporters to ask Henderson "if he could spell M-V-P." Bradshaw had just won the Super Bowl's award as well.

Pittsburgh won again the next season, defeating the Los Angeles Rams 31–19 behind two more touchdown passes from Bradshaw. One of them was a 73-yard strike to Stallworth with just over 12 minutes left that put the Steelers ahead for good. Bradshaw never played in another Super Bowl, but he had set the standard for quarterbacks on football's biggest stage.

JOE COOL

Joe Montana had two nicknames in his NFL career. One of them was "Joe Cool" for his calm nature. The other was the "Comeback Kid." He lived up to both on one drive near the end of Super Bowl XXIII in January 1989. His San Francisco 49ers were trailing the Cincinnati Bengals 16–13 with 3:20 left. The 49ers were just about to start a drive from their own 8-yard line when Montana noticed his teammates were nervous. He pointed to the stands and said, "Look, isn't that John Candy?" Whether or not Montana had actually spotted the famous actor and comedian didn't matter. He loosened up the huddle. Twelve plays later, he drilled a game-winning 10-yard touchdown pass to receiver John Taylor with 34 seconds remaining.

Joe Montana was the first player to ever win the Super Bowl MVP Award three times.

Super Bowl XXIII was Montana's third win. His first had also come against the Bengals seven years earlier in Super Bowl XVI. His second came in Super Bowl XIX against the Miami Dolphins after the 1984 season. NFL fans came into the game expecting to see Miami's record-setting quarterback Dan Marino air it out against San Francisco. And Marino indeed threw for 318 yards, but Montana stole the show. His 331 passing yards set a Super Bowl record. He added three touchdown passes in a 38–16 win.

By Super Bowl XXIII, another quarterback had passed Montana's record, but the 49ers' quarterback took it back with 357 yards against the Bengals. San Francisco then went back to the Super

Bowl a year later. Facing the Denver Broncos, Montana had another memorable day. He completed 22 of 29 passes for 297 yards and a Super Bowl–record five touchdowns in a 55–10 romp. It was Montana's fourth and final Super Bowl, but he left quite a legacy. At the time, his 83 completions, 1,142 passing yards, and 11 touchdowns were all the most in Super Bowl history.

THE WINNER

Tom Brady began the 2001 NFL season as a backup for the New England Patriots. The unknown sixth-round draft pick in 2000 only took over when New England's All-Pro starter Drew Bledsoe was injured in September. But Brady played so well that he kept the job even when Bledsoe came back. And after he led the Patriots on a game-winning drive in Super Bowl XXXVI to defeat the heavily favored St. Louis Rams, Brady was a star.

Before the 2001 season, the Patriots had never won a Super Bowl. With Brady running the offense, they won three in four years. The New England dynasty then spent 10 seasons coming close to a fourth championship. In Super Bowl XLIX in February 2015, Brady led New England to victory again, touching off a streak of three victories in the next five years.

Brady's six titles were incredible, but even more amazing was how he won them. Brady had a knack for coming up big late in close championship games. Two years after his late-game heroics against the Rams, Brady was at it again in Super Bowl XXXVIII. His last-minute, game-winning drive pushed the Patriots past the Carolina Panthers 32–29. A year later, Brady's two touchdown passes helped New England tip the Philadelphia Eagles 24–21.

Super Bowl XLIX was a 28–24 win over the Seattle Seahawks, but Brady's finest hour came in Super Bowl LI in February 2017. Down 28–3 to the Atlanta Falcons in the third quarter, Brady led four scoring drives in the final 17 minutes to tie the game. He then marched the Patriots down the field in overtime to win 34–28.

In his 10 Super Bowl appearances, Tom Brady threw 21 touchdown passes and only six interceptions.

Even after winning his sixth Super Bowl in February 2019, Brady's critics tried to argue that he only won because of New England's genius head coach, Bill Belichick. Brady proved them wrong after signing with the Tampa Bay Buccaneers in 2020. In his first season, Brady led the Bucs to a 31–9 demolition of the Kansas City Chiefs in Super Bowl LV. The 43-year-old quarterback threw three touchdown passes and was named the game's MVP for a fifth time.

Among Brady's Super Bowl records are those for total touchdown passes and MVPs. But perhaps his most impressive accomplishment was winning the big game seven times. Not only is that total the most of any NFL player, it's also more than any team has won.

THE COMEBACK KID

Brady's Buccaneers routed Kansas City in Super Bowl LV by frustrating Chiefs

ELWAY FINALLY WINS

Denver Broncos quarterback John Elway led the team to three Super Bowls in four years in the late 1980s. Denver was thumped each time. The team didn't make it back until Super Bowl XXXII after the 1997 season. The 37-year-old Elway led a gutsy performance in an emotional 31–24 victory over the Green Bay Packers. Elway led the Broncos to another Super Bowl win the next season.

quarterback Patrick Mahomes. It was a rare postseason loss for Mahomes. In his first seven seasons, he was 15–3 in the playoffs.

With a rifle arm and a knack for throwing passes few other quarterbacks would ever try, Mahomes is a human highlight reel. But in the Super Bowl, Mahomes has often shown his mental toughness, too. In each of Kansas City's three Super Bowl wins with Mahomes at the helm, he guided the team back from 10-point deficits.

The first came against the San Francisco 49ers in Super Bowl LIV in February 2020. Trailing 20–10 with 7:13 left, and facing third-and-15, Mahomes evaded the 49ers pressure and lofted a 44-yard pass to wide receiver Tyreek Hill. Four plays later, he hit tight end Travis Kelce on a one-yard touchdown pass. Mahomes added another touchdown pass as part of a 21-point fourth quarter and a 31–20 win.

Mahomes also has sneaky scrambling ability. With 170 yards in four appearances, he became the all-time leading rusher among Super Bowl quarterbacks. The Chiefs were back at Super Bowl LVII after the 2022 season. Mahomes entered the game nursing an ankle injury suffered earlier in the playoffs. He then led Kansas City back from 10 points down at halftime. With the score tied 35–35 and 2:55 left, Mahomes put aside his pain and scrambled 26 yards to the Philadelphia Eagles' 17-yard line. The clutch scramble helped set up the game-winning field goal.

One year later, Mahomes's Chiefs were facing the 49ers once again. And again Kansas City fell behind. But Mahomes rose to the

Patrick Mahomes, *center*, breaks away from two Philadelphia Eagles defenders on his key 26-yard fourth-quarter scramble in Super Bowl LVII in February 2023.

challenge once more. He threw for 333 yards and led the Chiefs with 66 more on the ground. And he capped the game with a one-yard touchdown pass to win it 25–22 in overtime. Though he was only 28 when the game ended, Mahomes had already achieved the status of Super Bowl legend.

32
12

SUPER RUNNING BACKS

Super Bowl IX in January 1975 was a defensive struggle. At halftime, the Pittsburgh Steelers led the Minnesota Vikings 2–0. But after Minnesota's Bill Brown fumbled the opening kickoff of the second half, the Steelers took over at the Vikings' 30-yard line. Pittsburgh head coach Chuck Noll knew just who to turn to. It was time to give the ball to Franco Harris.

The 6-foot, 2-inch, 230-pound running back put together a Hall of Fame career in the 1970s and 1980s by grinding out tough yards. Harris could be both graceful and physical on the same play. On the second snap of the drive, he took the handoff from quarterback Terry Bradshaw and ran to the left. Harris then spotted an opening back up the middle. He planted his foot and shimmied through the open space. That left him one-on-one with Minnesota's

Franco Harris bursts through a hole in the Dallas Cowboys' defense during Super Bowl XIII after the 1978 season.

star safety Paul Krause. Harris threw out his right arm and shoved Krause away while cutting back outside. He ended up with 24 yards before being run out of bounds at the 6-yard line.

Two plays later, Harris scored to make it 8–0. That touchdown held up as the key play of a 16–6 Steelers win. Harris's hard-charging running was on display all game. He carried the ball 34 times for 158 yards. Both were Super Bowl records at the time. After the game, Harris was named the game's MVP. He was the first Black player to ever win the award.

Harris never topped 100 yards again in the Super Bowl. But he was still a huge part of three Pittsburgh victories later in the decade. Thirty years after he retired, Harris's 101 career carries and 354 career yards were still Super Bowl records.

DUAL THREAT

In the 1980s, the San Francisco 49ers dominated the NFL with their West Coast offense. The strategy called for a lot of short passes. Running backs in the system had to be good receivers. Roger Craig was a perfect fit.

Craig was a high school hurdler, and he became known for his unique running style. He would pump his knees incredibly high. Though he wasn't the biggest back, that style of running made him tough to take down in the open field. When Craig caught passes out of the backfield, he was a nightmare for defenses.

Roger Craig makes a one-handed catch early in Super Bowl XIX on January 20, 1985, against the Miami Dolphins.

The Miami Dolphins found that out in Super Bowl XIX in January 1985. Craig rushed for 15 yards for 58 yards and a touchdown. He also caught seven passes for 77 yards and two scores. No player had ever scored three touchdowns in the same Super Bowl before.

Craig's final touchdown was a 16-yard reception with 6:38 left in the third quarter. Craig caught the pass in the left flat. He had a clear path to the end zone to make the score 37–16. Sensing victory was close, Craig high-stepped over the goal line.

Roger Craig had 198 rushing yards and 212 receiving yards in his three Super Bowls.

Craig helped the 49ers win two more Super Bowls. In his three appearances, he piled up 410 total yards from scrimmage. And his 20 career receptions were a Super Bowl record at the time.

THE EMMITT SMITH SHOW

The Dallas Cowboys had several stars when they ruled the NFL in the early 1990s. Troy Aikman was a steady, accurate quarterback. Wide receiver Michael Irvin was a brash talker who backed it up with spectacular play on the field. But when the going got tough for the Cowboys, they looked to the man wearing the No. 22 jersey. That meant handing the ball to Emmitt Smith.

Some considered Smith too short and slow for the NFL when he was drafted in 1989. They were quickly proved wrong. At 5 feet, 9 inches and 222 pounds, Smith used his tank-like legs to barrel straight ahead, often running through would-be tacklers. He retired in 2003 as the league's all-time leading rusher. And he also left his mark on the Super Bowl three times.

Smith rushed for 108 yards on 22 carries in Super Bowl XXVII after the 1992 season. But his only touchdown came long after Dallas's 52–17 rout over the Buffalo Bills was already decided. It was

TOUGH IN DEFEAT

Thurman Thomas's Buffalo Bills lost four consecutive Super Bowls in the early 1990s. But the team's star running back still piled up some impressive numbers. His 204 career rushing yards were tied for third-most all-time when he played in his last Super Bowl in January 1994. He also caught 20 Super Bowl passes and rushed for a score in each of his four games.

Emmitt Smith led the NFL in rushing each year the Dallas Cowboys won the Super Bowl in the 1990s.

a year later, in the rematch, that Smith rose to the status of Super Bowl legend.

The Bills bottled up Smith in the first half of the game, holding the Dallas running back to just 33 yards. The game was tied 13–13 with 13:14 left in the third quarter when the Cowboys took over at their own 36-yard line. Head coach Jimmy Johnson gave the ball to Smith on seven of the next eight plays. Smith rewarded his coaches by piling up 61 yards. He capped the drive by slipping a tackle in the backfield and weaving 15 yards for the go-ahead touchdown. Smith added a second score in the fourth quarter. He was named the MVP of Dallas's 30–13 victory.

Smith added two more rushing touchdowns two years later in a 27–17 win over the Steelers in Super Bowl XXX. Twenty years after he retired, Smith still held a Super Bowl record. No one had passed his five career rushing touchdowns in football's biggest game.

A HEADACHE FOR DEFENSES

Denver Broncos running back Terrell Davis has dealt with migraines his entire life. Before games, he used a special medication to make sure he was pain-free on the field. But ahead of Super Bowl XXXII in January 1998 against the Green Bay Packers, Davis forgot to take it.

Sure enough, a nasty migraine popped up during the game that wouldn't go away. Davis fought with poor vision all night. Early in the second quarter, the Broncos had the ball at the Green Bay 1-yard line.

Terrell Davis (30) bears down on a Green Bay Packers defender during Super Bowl XXXII in January 1998.

Davis, barely able to see, came to the sidelines. Head coach Mike Shanahan sent his star runner back to the field. The coach wasn't going to give him the ball, but he knew the Packers would be worried about Davis in that spot. The decoy worked. Quarterback John Elway sneaked over the line to tie the game 14–14.

That was one of the few times Davis didn't get the ball during the game. He fought through the headaches for 157 yards and three touchdowns on 30 punishing carries. His final score, a one-yard plunge with 1:47 left, put Denver up for good 31–24.

Davis was named the MVP of Super Bowl XXXII. A year later, he ran for another 102 yards as Denver beat the Atlanta Falcons 34–19. Davis was just the third player to rush for more than 100 yards in back-to-back Super Bowls.

In addition to his 102 rushing yards in Super Bowl XXXIII, Davis also caught two passes for 50 yards.

CHAPTER THREE

RECEIVING THREATS

The Pittsburgh Steelers of the 1970s were known for their hard-nosed play and even tougher players. Center Mike Webster was called "Iron Mike." Defensive lineman Joe Greene's nickname stuck so well that most football fans know him as "Mean" Joe Greene. Middle linebacker Jack Lambert was missing his two front teeth.

However, one offensive star didn't seem to fit the mold. Receiver Lynn Swann was graceful. When not on the field, he took ballet classes to perfect his footwork. Other players teased him for his off-season hobby, but few could keep up with him in the secondary.

Swann's amazing coordination was on full display in Super Bowl X in January 1976. Midway through the second quarter, Pittsburgh quarterback Terry Bradshaw heaved a pass down the right sideline.

Lynn Swann hurdles over Dallas Cowboys cornerback Mark Washington to make one of his famous catches in Super Bowl X.

Swann leaped high over the head of Dallas Cowboys cornerback Mark Washington to snag the pass, then toe-tapped the sideline to stay in bounds on his way down. The play went for 32 yards.

Swann proved he could also juggle in the third quarter. He and Washington were stride for stride in the middle of the field as Bradshaw heaved another deep ball. Both Swann and Washington went for it, and the ball bobbled in the air as they came down. Swann kept his balance and barely avoided landing on Washington as the cornerback lay on the ground. Swann then snagged the ball out of the air as he stumbled to the turf for a 53-yard gain.

Swann ended the game with four catches. His fourth was a 64-yard haul for a touchdown in the fourth quarter. After the game, he danced away with the MVP Award.

Swann played in two more Super Bowls for Pittsburgh, and he caught a touchdown pass in each game. He left the NFL in 1982 holding the Super Bowl record with 364 receiving yards. But it was his skills and grace in Super Bowl X that fans still remember.

TWO-MAN SHOW

Lynn Swann wasn't the Pittsburgh Steelers' only big receiving threat in the 1970s. John Stallworth also made his fair share of big plays. Stallworth caught two Super Bowl touchdown passes of 70 yards or more in his career. Stallworth's average of 24.4 yards per reception in Super Bowl play is still a record.

RICE IS COOKING

The San Francisco 49ers routed the Miami Dolphins 38–16 in Super Bowl XIX. The 49ers threw for 331 yards in the January 1985 game, and the greatest receiver in NFL history had yet to join the team. Three months later, San Francisco drafted Jerry Rice with the 16th pick in the NFL Draft.

Jerry Rice sprints away from two Denver Broncos defenders on his way to the end zone in Super Bowl XXIV after the 1989 season.

Rice is the only NFL player to ever catch three touchdown passes in a Super Bowl, a feat he accomplished twice.

Rice quickly became a star, but it took until his fourth season for the 49ers to reach the big game again. Rice didn't waste any time writing his name in Super Bowl lore. In Super Bowl XXIII, he racked up a then-Super Bowl record of 11 receptions. His 215 receiving yards were also a record, as he was named the game's MVP. The 49ers defeated the Cincinnati Bengals 20–16.

As impressive as that performance was, it was simply a warm-up for Rice. San Francisco returned to the Super Bowl a year later to face the Denver Broncos. Less than five minutes into the game, Rice hauled in a 20-yard touchdown pass from quarterback Joe Montana.

Rice's biggest weapon was his blazing speed. With 40 seconds left in the first half, he cruised past the Denver secondary. Montana found him wide open for a 38-yard touchdown strike.

The game was a historic 55–10 blowout, with Rice adding a third touchdown catch early in the third quarter. It was a record-setting fourth career touchdown reception. In two games, he had become one of the Super Bowl's greatest players. But Rice was far from done.

In January 1995, Rice and the 49ers returned to the Super Bowl. This time they had a new quarterback, lefty Steve Young. Once again, Rice went to work early. He split the San Diego Chargers defense for a 44-yard touchdown pass from Young on the game's third offensive play. Rice capped the 49–26 win with two more touchdown catches in the second half. His final total was 10 catches for 149 yards and three scores.

Rice capped his Super Bowl career in 2002 after moving to the Oakland Raiders. Even at 39 years old, he was still a factor. Oakland lost the game, but Rice caught five passes for 77 yards and his eighth Super Bowl touchdown. Two decades after he retired, he was still the all-time Super Bowl leader in receptions, yards, and touchdowns.

GRONK

Tight ends weren't always a big factor on offense for NFL teams. For decades, they were blockers first and pass catchers second. But that changed in the 2000s as a new crop of hyper-athletic big men started playing the position. Few were more physically gifted than Rob Gronkowski.

The fun-loving 6-foot, 6-inch, 255-pounder nicknamed "Gronk" played 11 NFL seasons for the New England Patriots and Tampa Bay Buccaneers. He appeared in the Super Bowl in nearly half of them. And Gronkowski was a major factor in his five appearances. Catching passes from Tom Brady, Gronkowski hauled in 29 Super Bowl receptions for 364 career yards. His five touchdowns trail only Jerry Rice for the most all-time.

However, Gronkowski's impact goes beyond his stats. Just his terrifying presence on the field opened up space for his teams' other offensive weapons. Brady and Gronkowski played in five Super Bowls together, winning four. In those games, Brady threw for 1,862 yards and 12 touchdowns.

Rob Gronkowski celebrates a touchdown with his trademark spike during Super Bowl LV in February 2021.

ALL EYES ON KELCE

Fans have long been drawn to Kansas City Chiefs tight end Travis Kelce. Beyond his great athleticism and soft hands, he also displayed a more relatable side off the field. After winning the Super Bowl in February 2023, Kelce hosted the popular TV show *Saturday Night Live*. The following season, his relationship with pop music superstar Taylor Swift made national news. Cameras seemed to follow him everywhere.

However, Kelce gets the most attention for his ability to come up with big plays when needed most. With under a minute remaining in Super Bowl LVIII after the 2023 season, Kansas City trailed San Francisco 19–16. The Chiefs were facing third-and-7 at the 49ers' 33-yard line.

Head coach Andy Reid called a play that had Kelce cut across the middle of the field just beyond the line of scrimmage. Quarterback Patrick Mahomes hit Kelce in stride. The 250-pound tight end outraced three defenders for a 22-yard gain. Kicker Harrison Butker kicked the tying field goal two plays later.

The Chiefs went on to win 25–22 in overtime. Kelce hauled in nine passes for 93 yards. At the end of the game, he had passed Gronkowski for the most receptions by a tight end in Super Bowl history. His 31 catches were only two shy of Jerry Rice's all-time record. It was also his third Super Bowl win in four tries.

Travis Kelce caught six passes for 43 yards and a touchdown in Super Bowl LIV after the 2019 season. Kansas City defeated the San Francisco 49ers 31–20.

TON
13

DEFENSIVE AND SPECIAL TEAMS STANDOUTS

The Kansas City Chiefs' Harrison Butker drilled a 29-yard field goal to tie Super Bowl LVIII at 19–19 with three seconds left. The Chiefs went on to win the February 2024 game in overtime. And for the second year in a row Butker had booted a successful field goal with the Super Bowl on the line. At only 28 years old, Butker already had nine successful field goals in Super Bowl play, an all-time record. And he was just the latest in a long line of defensive and special teams players to make their mark on football's biggest game.

Fifty years before Butker's heroics, Jake Scott anchored the Miami Dolphins' stalwart defensive unit. The group was nicknamed the "No-Name" defense because they seemingly didn't have any stars. But Scott stepped up in the season's biggest game two straight years.

Jake Scott races out of the end zone after making one of his two interceptions in Super Bowl VII on January 14, 1973.

The Dolphins went 14–0 during the 1972 regular season. After two playoff wins, they faced Washington with a chance to become the first undefeated Super Bowl champions. Scott made sure the defense held up its end of the bargain. He picked off Washington quarterback Billy Kilmer early in the second quarter. Scott did it again late in the fourth quarter with Miami holding a 14–0 lead. Neither of Scott's picks led to points for the Dolphins. But his effort was key to a 14–7 win that wrapped up Miami's perfect 17–0 season. After the game, he was named the Super Bowl's MVP.

The next year, Miami returned to the Super Bowl to face the Minnesota Vikings. The Dolphins were up 17–0 late in the second quarter when Minnesota put together a drive. On a fourth-and-1 play from the Dolphins' 6-yard line, Minnesota's Oscar Reed fumbled. Scott pounced on the ball to kill the Vikings' hopes of getting points on the board before halftime. In the second half, Miami cruised to a 24–7 win.

SACK ARTIST

The San Francisco 49ers took a 20–16 lead on a touchdown pass with just 34 seconds left in Super Bowl XXIII. But the Cincinnati Bengals still had time for a miracle in the January 1989 game. On second-and-5 from the Cincinnati 31-yard line, Bengals quarterback Boomer Esiason rolled to his left. Waiting for him was 49ers defensive end Charles Haley, who wrapped up Esiason for a sack.

Two desperation passes followed, which were both incomplete. Haley's takedown effectively wrapped up the win for the 49ers.

It was Haley's second sack of the game, and his first Super Bowl win. It would not be his last of either statistic. Haley's 49ers won again in Super Bowl XXIV after the 1989 season.

Charles Haley (94) puts a hit on Cincinnati Bengals quarterback Boomer Esiason in Super Bowl XXIII after the 1988 season.

PAST SACK MASTER

Sacks didn't become an official NFL statistic for individual players until 1982. But researchers for Pro Football Reference went back and reviewed old Super Bowls. They determined that Pittsburgh Steelers defensive end L. C. Greenwood had five sacks in Pittsburgh's four victories during the 1970s. However, the website's research is not recognized by the NFL. Charles Haley is still considered the official record holder.

In 1992, Haley was traded to the Dallas Cowboys. He arrived just in time to help put Dallas over the top. The following January, the Cowboys faced the Buffalo Bills in Super Bowl XXVII. With the game tied 7–7 late in the first quarter, Haley sacked Buffalo quarterback Jim Kelly at the Bills' 2-yard line. The ball popped loose straight into the arms of Cowboys defensive lineman Jimmie Jones. Jones fell into the end zone for a touchdown. The play helped turn the game in Dallas's favor. The Cowboys rolled through the second half. They eventually won 52–17.

That win set up the Cowboys as the league's new dynasty. Dallas won two of the next three Super Bowls as well. Haley picked up at least 1/2 of a sack in each game. His 4 1/2 career sacks set the official Super Bowl record. By the time he left the team in 1996, Haley had won five Super Bowls in eight years. Until Tom Brady passed him, Haley had the most championship rings of any NFL player. He still holds the record for defensive players. No other NFL defender even has four.

Haley's strip of Buffalo quarterback Jim Kelly was a key defensive play in Super Bowl XXVII on January 31, 1993.

HEART AND SOUL

The Baltimore Ravens reached Super Bowl XXXV in January 2001 on the back of one of the best defenses ever to line up on an NFL field. The team had shut out four opponents during the regular season. The Ravens held three others to only a field goal, including two of their three playoff opponents. Ray Lewis, Baltimore's hard-hitting, trash-talking middle linebacker, was the team's heart. "Ray Lewis is the greatest leader in team sports history," said teammate Shannon Sharpe. "No one is even close."

Lewis was a monster on the field in the Super Bowl against the New York Giants. He led the team with five tackles. Lewis flew all over the place to hit Giants players.

Middle linebackers generally don't defend passes that often, but Lewis was an exception. He tipped or knocked down four of Giants quarterback Kerry Collins's attempts. One of Lewis's tips, in the second quarter, ended up as an interception by Baltimore linebacker Jamie Sharper. After the game, Lewis was named the MVP of Baltimore's 34–7 romp. He was the first defensive player to win the award since Super Bowl XX in 1986.

Lewis was still at it with the Ravens in 2012. Even at 37 years old, he was still impacting games. Though he missed most of the regular season with a torn biceps, Lewis returned to lead all NFL players with 51 postseason tackles. Five of them came in Super Bowl XLVII as Baltimore outlasted the 49ers 34–31. He retired after the game as a two-time winner.

FOR THE WIN

Adam Vinatieri was an unlikely NFL star. He grew up in South Dakota and starred as a kicker in college at lower-level South Dakota State.

Ray Lewis salutes Baltimore fans after the Ravens won Super Bowl XXXV in January 2001.

He then spent a year playing for a team in Europe before the New England Patriots gave him a shot in 1996. He retired 24 years later as the NFL's all-time leading scorer. But he is best remembered for two huge moments in the Super Bowl.

In February 2002, the Patriots were huge underdogs in Super Bowl XXXVI against the St. Louis Rams and their high-powered offense. But the Patriots hung in, and with a few minutes left to play the game was tied 17–17. Quarterback Tom Brady guided New England in position for a game-winning 48-yard field goal with seven seconds left.

Never before had a Super Bowl ended on a last-play, game-winning field goal. But Vinatieri had already proved he could be a clutch kicker. Three weeks earlier, he had kicked a 45-yard game-tying field goal against the Oakland Raiders in a snowstorm. This time, he was kicking indoors at the New Orleans Superdome. And he split the uprights for a 20–17 victory.

Any kicker would hope for one chance to win a Super Bowl with a kick like Vinatieri's. But no one would ever expect two chances to do it in their career. However, two years later, the Patriots were tied 29–29 against the Carolina Panthers in Super Bowl XXXVIII with 1:13 left. Brady moved Vinatieri into position again with nine seconds remaining. This time, the Patriots kicker nailed a 41-yard attempt. The kick cemented Vinatieri's legacy as one of the most clutch players in Super Bowl history.

Adam Vinatieri won three Super Bowls as a member of the New England Patriots and a fourth while playing for the Indianapolis Colts.

HONORABLE MENTIONS

HARRISON BUTKER

The Chiefs' kicker booted a last-second game winner in Super Bowl LVII against the Philadelphia Eagles in 2023. A year later, he kicked the longest field goal in Super Bowl history with a 57-yard kick against the 49ers. His nine field goals are also a Super Bowl record.

LARRY CSONKA

"Zonk" was the punishing heart of the Miami Dolphins' ground attack for back-to-back wins in Super Bowls VII and VIII during the early 1970s. Csonka rushed for more than 100 yards in each game.

MICHAEL IRVIN

Irvin was the Cowboys' biggest deep threat for their dynasty run of the 1990s. In three Super Bowls, Irvin caught 16 passes for 256 yards and two touchdowns, both in Super Bowl XXVII after the 1992 season.

PEYTON MANNING

Manning had to wait nearly 10 years for his first Super Bowl win before guiding the Indianapolis Colts to victory in Super Bowl XLI after the 2006 season. The record-setting quarterback added another victory after the 2015 season as a member of the Denver Broncos.

Peyton Manning

Deion Sanders

ANDRE REED

Reed never won a Super Bowl with the Buffalo Bills, playing on four consecutive losing teams in the early 1990s. But the wide receiver caught at least five passes in each game. His 27 career Super Bowl receptions and 323 yards both rank among the all-time leaders.

JOHN RIGGINS

Washington's 230-pound "Big Rig" was another bruising runner. In Super Bowl XVII in January 1983, he ran over, around, and through the Miami Dolphins for 166 yards and a key touchdown on a Super Bowl–record 38 carries.

DEION SANDERS

Sanders won back-to-back Super Bowls after the 1994 and 1995 seasons with two different teams. The first came with the San Francisco 49ers. The second came with the Dallas Cowboys. The cornerback also played some offense and had a 47-yard reception in Super Bowl XXX.

KURT WARNER

Warner won only one Super Bowl in his career. He was named MVP of Super Bowl XXXIV in 2000 as he led the upstart St. Louis Rams to victory. But his 1,156 career Super Bowl passing yards over three appearances were second to Tom Brady when Warner retired in 2009.

GLOSSARY

biceps
A large muscle in the front of the upper arm.

clutch
Performing well in an important situation that often decides a competition or game.

dynasty
A team that has an extended period of success, usually winning multiple championships in the process.

flat
The area of the field near the line of scrimmage and the sideline.

migraine
A powerful headache that can cause nausea and affect vision.

retired
Ended one's career.

rout
One team or individual defeating another badly.

sack
A tackle of the quarterback behind the line of scrimmage before he can pass the ball.

secondary
The defensive players—cornerbacks and safeties—who start the play farthest from the line.

stalwart
Strong or tough.

MORE INFORMATION

Books

Graves, Will. *GOATs of Football*. Abdo, 2022.

Hanlon, Luke. *Football Strategies*. Abdo, 2024.

Stathes, Corbu. *Everything Football*. Abdo, 2025.

Online Resources

To learn more about Super Bowl stars, please visit **abdobooklinks.com** or scan this QR code. These links are routinely monitored and updated to provide the most current information available.

INDEX

About the Author

David J. Clarke is a freelance sportswriter. Originally from Helena, Montana, he now lives in Savannah, Georgia.